Hamster relations

Hamsters, like mice and gerbils, belong to an animal family called rodents. Rodents have front teeth which continue to grow all through their life.

Hamsters gnaw at things. This stops their front teeth from getting too long.

Night life

Hamsters are nocturnal. This means that they sleep in the day and get up at night. This may be because in the wild there are fewer enemies around at night.

Sniff...
Sniff...

You can try to train your hamster to get up in the early evening.

Hearing

Hamsters have very good hearing and do not like sudden or loud noises. Your hamster will soon learn to recognize you by the sound of your voice.

Loud noises frighten hamsters, so keep your pet's cage in a quiet place.

DO NOT DISTURB

Smelling

Hamsters recognize things by how they smell rather than how they look. Your hamster will know you by your smell as well as your voice.

Let your new hamster sniff your hand so it can get to know you by becoming used to your smell.

Sniff...
Sniff...

Eyesight

Hamsters have poor eyesight. If you stood more than about four steps away from one, it would probably not see you. They see best in dim light.

Whiskers

A hamster uses its whiskers as feelers. They tell it if an object is nearby, or if a space is wide enough to get through.

Hamsters twitch their whiskers to sense movement around them.

This hamster measured the tube with its whiskers before crawling through.

Types of hamsters

You may be able to choose from different types of hamsters when you are buying your pet. The most common pet hamster is the Syrian hamster. The other types are all known as dwarf hamsters, because they are so small.

Syrian hamsters

Syrian hamsters can be short-haired or long-haired. They are sometimes called golden hamsters. They all used to be golden, but now come in other shades too.

Syrian hamsters can be a variety of shades, from white to dark brown.

Short-haired Syrians, like this one, look smaller than long-haired ones because they have less fur.

This is a long-haired Syrian.

These hamsters are nicknamed "teddy bears" because they look so cuddly.

Historic hamsters

Syrian hamsters were once thought to be extinct. Then, in 1930, a nest of 11 babies and their mother were discovered in some wheatfields in Syria. Syrian hamsters first became popular as pets in America.

Almost all pet Syrian hamsters today are descended from one family found in a Syrian field.

Dwarf hamsters

Dwarf hamsters are less than half the size of Syrians and so can be a little more awkward to handle.

Campbell's Russian, or Djungarian, hamsters are one of the most common types of dwarfs to be kept as pets.

Campbell's Russian, or Djungarian, hamsters have round bodies. ⟍--➜

Some other popular types of dwarf hamsters that are kept as pets are Winter White, or Siberian, hamsters, Chinese hamsters and Roborovski hamsters.

This is a Winter White, or Siberian, hamster.

Roborovski hamsters are the smallest hamsters.

One or two?

Syrian hamsters live alone in the wild, so you must keep a Syrian hamster in a cage on its own.

PRIVATE

Dwarf hamsters live in family groups in the wild. You may be able to keep two dwarfs together, unless they fight.

Dwarf hamsters can be kept in same-sex pairs or small groups. Don't mix species.

11

Hamster homes

Before you buy a hamster, decide what type of home to get for it. It will need as big a home as possible, so it has room to run around.

Tanks

Tanks are suitable for dwarf hamsters but not Syrians. Dwarfs tend to stay on one level more than Syrians and don't climb up bars.

A tank needs slits in the lid to let air in.

Bar cages

A hamster will use the bars of a cage for climbing and gnawing. Bar cages also allow the hamster to get plenty of air. You can find out what to put inside a cage on pages 16-19.

For dwarf hamsters, the bars of the cage must be no more than 9mm ($\frac{3}{8}$in) apart, or the hamsters may squeeze through.

A hamster may enjoy running up and down different levels in the cage and climbing on its horizontal bars.

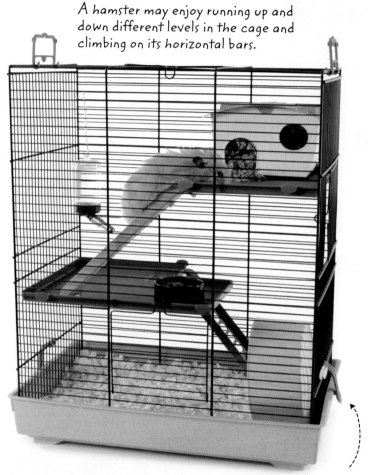

A cage with a deep-sided tray at the bottom will stop the hamster from pushing out wood shavings (see page 16).

Make sure the doors fasten securely. Hamsters are very good at escaping.

Labyrinths

Cages like this, with a network of rooms and tunnels, are a little like the burrows where hamsters live in the wild. These cages are expensive but you can start off with just a few units and add to them gradually.

For dwarfs, you would need to add ladders or have a bungalow arrangement. Dwarfs cannot climb up vertical tubes.

Slits and small holes in the units allow the hamster to get air.

Many hamsters
enjoy climbing
up and down
to rooms on
different levels.

Burrows

In the wild, hamsters
live underground
in burrows like this
one. Tunnels lead to
different rooms and
up to ground level.

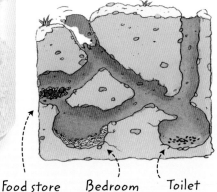

Food store   Bedroom   Toilet

What will I need?

Buy the things your hamster will need before you bring your new pet home. You can find everything in a good pet store.

Wood shavings

Buy a bag of wood shavings. Spread some at least 25mm (1in) deep on the floor of the cage. Fine sawdust can harm hamsters.

Hamsters dig burrows in the wild and need to dig around in their cage too.

Bedding

Buy soft hay or shredded paper bedding. The fluffy type may harm your hamster if it eats it. You can add torn up paper, such as paper towel, too, but it must be pale and plain.

Put a couple of handfuls of bedding in the cage.

Hamsters enjoy making their own beds.

16

Bottle

For water, your hamster needs a drip-feed bottle which attaches to the cage. Put it away from the bedding in case it drips.

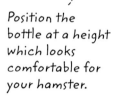

Position the bottle at a height which looks comfortable for your hamster.

Dish

An earthenware dish, like this one, is best for food, because it will be too heavy for your hamster to knock over.

A hamster will chew on a plastic food dish, but not on an earthenware one.

Your hamster may take its paper or hay bedding into its nest.

Nest

In their burrows, hamsters sleep safely right out of sight. Your hamster will probably like to sleep in a special house or nest in its cage. Check that the house will still be big enough when your hamster is full grown.

Toys

You can buy your hamster toys, but don't clutter up the cage with them. Try putting them out for your hamster when it is running free (see page 44). Never try to force your hamster to play with a toy.

Hamsters enjoy toilet roll and paper towel tubes as much as bought toys.

Exercise wheel

Your hamster needs a wheel to get exercise. Fix it close to the bars of the cage, so the hamster can't get trapped behind it.

The wheel should be solid, so the hamster can't get its legs trapped.

A long-haired Syrian will need a large wheel.

Buying a hamster

It is best to buy a hamster from a pet store or a hamster breeder. Buy from a place where the animals look clean and well cared for.

Which one?

Choose a healthy hamster that is lively and curious. Ask to see it handled and don't buy it if it is very frightened or bites.

This is a healthy Syrian hamster.

Its eyes should be bright, with no stickiness.

Look for a plump body.

Check that its nose and mouth are dry.

Look for a thick, silky coat with no blemishes.

Male or female?

Both males and females make good pets. Don't buy a female from a cage with males in it. She may be pregnant. Females can become pregnant at only four weeks old and males can father babies at four weeks.

Ask the staff to check the hamster's sex.

How old?

Your hamster should be between five and eight weeks old when you buy it. Hamsters are easier to tame when they are young.

Baby hamsters don't usually fight, so they are kept together at the pet store.

Getting home

Your hamster will be put in a box. Ask to take a little of its bedding for its new cage, so it will feel more at home. Go straight home.

The hamster may try to chew its way out of the box.

Settling in

Your hamster may be frightened. Place the box in its cage and let it come out when it's ready. Put the top on, then leave it alone for a few hours.

Put the box on the floor of the cage.

Let your hamster leave its box in its own time — don't try to force it out.

The ideal spot

Hamsters feel comfortable at the same temperature as humans. There are a few places where you should not put your hamster's cage. Keep it away from:

- radiators and fires
- direct sunlight
- windows and doors
- damp places
- televisions and stereos
- other pets

You may not get much sleep if you keep your hamster in your bedroom.

slurp, slurp...

scratch, scratch...

whirr, whirrr...

Feeding your hamster

To stay healthy, your hamster needs a combination of dried hamster food from a pet store, fresh fruit and vegetables, and water.

Dried food

Most hamster food is a mixture like the one shown here. This is the type of food hamsters eat in the wild. In some countries, people give hamsters food pellets and food blocks too.

Store the food in a cool place, in an airtight container. Don't keep it for more than three months.

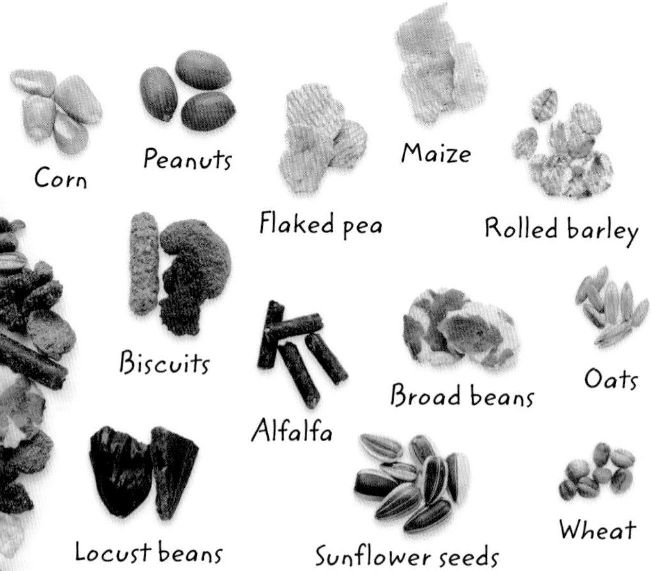

Corn

Peanuts

Flaked pea

Maize

Rolled barley

Biscuits

Alfalfa

Broad beans

Oats

Locust beans

Sunflower seeds

Wheat

How much and when?

A Syrian hamster needs about a tablespoon of dried food mix a day. A dwarf will eat a little less. If you give pellets, ask at the pet store what the correct amount is.

Try to feed your hamster at the same time every day. It may then get used to getting up at that time.

Your hamster may learn to anticipate food.

Hoarding food

In the wild, hamsters hoard their food in a store, in case supplies are hard to find later. Pets make food stores in their cages too.

Hamsters often make a food store near their bed.

Pouches

Hamsters have big pouches, like pockets, in their cheeks. In the wild, they fill their pouches with food to carry it back to the safety of their burrow. They empty their pouches by pushing the food out with their paws.

Your hamster will stuff its pouches with food, then carry it to the store in its cage.

The food stays dry inside the hamster's pouches.

Treats

You can buy your hamster various treats. Ask at the pet store how often you should give these.

Treat sticks can be hung from the bars of the cage.

Dry foods to avoid

There are several foods which will make a hamster unwell. Never give sweets, chocolate, salted snacks, salted nuts, or anything spicy or sticky.

Sharp, dry, stiff or sticky food can get stuck in the hamster's cheek pouches.

Fresh food

Hamsters need a small amount of fresh fruit or vegetables every day. You can give the fresh food at the same time as the dried hamster food. You will soon get to know which fruit and vegetables your hamster prefers.
If it doesn't like something, it won't eat it.

This hamster is enjoying eating a tomato.

Preparing the food

Before you give fruit or vegetables to your hamster, you need to wash them thoroughly in cold water, then dry them on a paper towel. Don't peel them or take out seeds, though. Your hamster will enjoy doing this itself.

Hamsters usually like these foods.

White cabbage

Carrot

Tomato

Cucumber

Apple

Grapes

Melon

Fresh foods to avoid

Don't give your hamster onions, garlic, oranges or other citrus fruits. These foods can make hamsters unwell. Only give lettuce or melon in tiny amounts.

Onions, garlic and peppers can cause an upset tummy.

29

How much to give

Give your hamster between 10 and 20g (about ½oz) of fresh fruits and vegetables a day. Any more will cause a tummy ache. Fresh food soon goes bad, so throw away any leftovers every day.

A hamster with a day's portion of carrot and grape

Water

Give your hamster fresh water every day. Don't worry if it doesn't drink much. It will get water from fruit and vegetables.

If bubbles rise to the top as your hamster drinks, the bottle is working.

Milk and yogurt

Hamsters can have very fresh milk or
live, natural, unsweetened yogurt. Throw
leftovers away next morning and wash
the dish very well.

*A teaspoonful of
yogurt, or about a
tablespoon of milk, is
enough for one day.*

*Put milk or yogurt
in a heavy dish.*

Vitamins and minerals

You can buy vitamin drops and
mineral stones for a hamster.
If yours is healthy and has
a good diet, it shouldn't
really need them.

*Extra vitamins and minerals may
be useful when your hamster is old.*

Keeping clean

Hamsters are very clean. They wash themselves all over several times a day and have mini-washes at other times, too.

Fur

A hamster's fur keeps it warm in the night-time cold. If a hamster keeps its fur neat and tidy, it will be warmer than if the fur is all tousled.

Clean fur helps to stop a hamster's body heat from escaping.

SHIVER...
SHIVER...

CHATTER...
CHATTER...

Scent glands

Syrian hamsters have a dark patch on each hip. These are scent glands.

RUB...
RUB...

Hamsters let out a smelly grease from their scent glands, as they rub against things. This marks the things as their property.

Washing routine

Hamsters wash quickly and energetically. They lick their front paws over and over again and use them as face cloths.

This hamster is washing the back of its neck.

Hamsters use their teeth to nibble out tangles in their fur.

If they can't reach a part of their body with their front paws, they use their back paws instead. Their claws make good combs.

Long hair tangles

Hamsters don't usually need any help with grooming. Just occasionally, a long-haired hamster may get a stubborn tangle in its fur.

You can tease this out using your fingers, a bristle toothbrush or a special hamster brush.

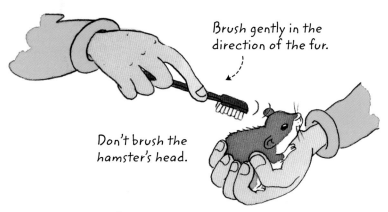

Brush gently in the direction of the fur.

Don't brush the hamster's head.

Open wide

Although you can't usually see them, hamsters have 12 teeth at the back of their mouth for chewing, as well as the four at the front.

YAWN...

Hamsters are one of the few animals who are born with a full set of teeth.

Healthy teeth

You need to give your hamster hard things to gnaw, or its front teeth will get too long. You can try carrots, an unshelled peanut, toilet roll and paper towel tubes, or a mineral stone or special gnawing block from a pet store.

Gnawing helps to clean the teeth, as well as keeping their length down.

This hamster is chewing a wooden gnawing block from a pet store.

What does it mean?

If you watch your hamster closely, you may be able to tell how it is feeling from some of the things it does.

Feeling sleepy

If your hamster's ears are folded back, it is a sign that it is sleepy. Don't try to play with it or it could get annoyed and bite.

This hamster has just woken up.

Leave a sleepy hamster alone until it is looking more alert.

Bed-making

Hamsters are good at making beds to suit the weather. They pile on bedding when it is cold, and spread it out when it is warm.

A bed for warm weather

A bed for cold weather

Sometimes your hamster may move its bed to a different part of its cage.

Toilet habits

Some hamsters are quite tidy and always pee in the same part of their cage, usually in a corner.

A hamster turns in circles when it wants to pee.

Hamsters sometimes keep their droppings in their food store and even eat them. Don't worry if your hamster does this.

...oh, yuk!

Feeling curious

If your hamster hears or smells something interesting, it will lift one of its front paws, or stand right up on its hind legs, ready to investigate. It will listen hard and sniff the air.

Hearing something interesting, this hamster has lifted its paw and pricked up its ears to listen.

Smelling something interesting, this hamster has stood up and is sniffing the air.

Feeling frightened

If a hamster is afraid, it may freeze quite still, or it may start washing very fast. It may creep along jerkily, its belly pressed to the ground and its tail up, or it may stand on its hind legs and bare its teeth.

If a hamster screeches, it is really frightened.

...SCREECH!

...SCREECH!

...SCREECH!

Gnawing the bars

If your hamster gnaws its cage bars, it may be bored and want to come out or it may be trying to wear its teeth down.

Try giving your hamster something else to gnaw (see page 35) and see if it stops gnawing the bars.

Taming your hamster

If you handle your hamster gently and patiently, it should become very tame. The sooner you begin, the easier taming will be. Start the day after you buy your hamster.

Try to handle your new hamster three or four times every day, but only for a few minutes at a time. You will need to have a grown-up to help you at first.

Time of day

Wait for your hamster to be wide awake and active. Give it time after getting up to go to the toilet, and have a snack and perhaps a wash.

When your hamster is feeling fully awake, its ears will prick up and it will start moving around its cage.

Getting prepared

Put your hamster's cage on the floor in a quiet room. Block off the area around it so the hamster can't escape. Take off the lid.

Keep all your movements slow and smooth while the cage lid is off.

Introducing yourself

Talk softly to your hamster, so it gets to know your voice. Then, offer it some food from your fingers and stroke it gently, so it gets to know your smell.

Hold food like this. One finger sticking out may get mistaken for food.

Picking your hamster up

Facing your hamster, so it can see you, cup your hands around it like this. Only lift it just off the cage floor.

Lift it slowly, keeping your movements smooth.

Try not to touch your hamster's head.

Move your hands to this position. If your hamster wriggles, let it get down and try again later.

Once you can pick your hamster up, take it out of its cage, and sit down to let it run from hand to hand.

Never drop your hamster. A fall from over 20cm (8in) may hurt it badly.

If it runs too fast for you, block its path like this, to slow it down. It will also enjoy climbing all over you.

You can check your hamster for lumps, scratches, or anything out of the ordinary while holding it.

Hold your hamster securely but not too tightly, or you will hurt it.

Avoiding bites

Hamsters only bite if they are frightened. Never tease your hamster. Don't poke things through the bars.

...SNIFF
...SNIFF

Don't pick your hamster up with the smell of food on your hands. Try not to make sudden, jerky movements.

Don't shout at your hamster or punish it, even if it does bite. This will only make it more likely to bite again.

43

Coming out to play

Your hamster will keep itself busy in its cage, but it is good for it to come out to play too. Once it is tame, it will probably enjoy playing with you best of all.

When to play

You should get your hamster out for only 10–15 minutes at a time, but you can get it out more than once in an evening. If it doesn't respond to its name and a gentle tap on the cage, let it sleep.

A hamster mustn't play for too long without a rest.

Running free

Your hamster will love to explore a room. Block off any escape routes. Watch your hamster all the time, for its own safety.

Make sure it doesn't gnaw anything
valuable, such as furniture.
Don't let it run free like
this until it is tame.

*Put out any toys you
have bought for
your hamster.*

Danger

Keep your hamster away from people's feet,
other pets, hot radiators, sofas, water, pipes,
fires, electric sockets and cables.

*Make sure no one
opens a door onto your
hamster. It could be badly hurt.*

Exercise balls

You can buy a ball for a hamster to run around in. Keep your pet in one for around 10–15 minutes a day. Let it out sooner if it shows signs of distress, such as washing quickly.

An exercise ball may be useful if it is not safe for your hamster to run free.

If the ball keeps coming open, put tape over its entrance.

Escapes

If your hamster escapes, try leaving its cage open on the floor nearby. It may come back for food and then curl up in bed.

Or, put strong-smelling food, such as cabbage, in a bucket with around 2.5cm (1in) of shavings and some bedding. Make steps with books.

Your hamster will be able to climb into the bucket but not out again.

If you aren't sure which room the hamster is in, put sunflower seeds in each one, then shut the doors. Do any of them disappear?

Put a certain number of seeds in one corner of each room.

Making a run

You can make a run for your hamster to play in when it is out of its cage. You can copy the run shown here, or make a simpler one.

This run is made out of tissue boxes, and toilet roll and paper towel tubes.

Safety first

A pale, plain box is safest.

Use pale tissue boxes and cardboard tubes, without much printing on them. Strong dyes may harm your hamster if it chews the cardboard.

Fit the run together without tape or glue. Tape may harm your hamster if it eats some. It is best to avoid even non-toxic glue.

If the boxes or tubes are stiff to cut, ask someone to help you.

It can be hard to get the point of your scissors through tough cardboard to start your cuts.

Tubes into boxes

To fit a tube into a box, position the tube on one side of the box, then draw around the end of it.

Cut out the circle. It may be easiest to make a hole in the middle of the circle first, then cut to the edge.

Push the tube into the hole. Slope it down, or leave it straight so your hamster has to climb into it.

Tubes into tubes

To fit tubes together, draw around the end of one onto paper. Cut out the circle.

Put only a small amount of glue on the circle.

Glue the circle onto the other tube, where you want the hole. Cut the circle out.

For a join like this, this tube needs to be quite wide.

Push the first tube into the hole. Leave room for your hamster to move.

Holes and slits

Cut holes in the top of some tubes. Make sure they are big enough for your hamster to squeeze through.

Cut slits in a tube, for your hamster to climb up. You don't need to cut exactly to the sizes shown here.

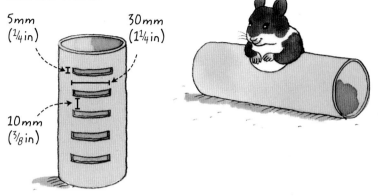

5mm (¼ in)

30mm (1¼ in)

10mm (⅜ in)

Hamsters enjoy rushing around in a run and popping up in different places.

Cleaning out

Hamsters don't like having their cages disturbed, but they need to be cleaned out once a week. You will need someone to help you at first. Wash your hands after cleaning.

When to clean out

Clean out your hamster when it is awake. If there's no one to play with it, put it in a deep, clean box, bucket or bin, while you clean.

Put shavings in a deep bucket and let your hamster burrow.

Leave a gap of at least 23cm (9in) between the rim and the shavings so the hamster can't climb out.

Every day

Give your hamster fresh water, and throw away any leftover fresh food before it starts to rot. Replace wet shavings where your hamster pees with fresh shavings.

Scoop up wet shavings with a paper towel or a scoop.

Wrap them in newspaper and throw them away.

Once a week

Empty out all the shavings, bedding and food. Keep half the bedding and a little dry food from the food store. It will comfort your hamster if you put these familiar things back into its clean cage.

Separate out some bedding and dried food.

53

Washing out

Use hot water and mild dishwashing liquid to wash the dish, bottle, house, wheel, and cage bottom. Wash the cage bars every few weeks.

Shake the bottle hard to loosen any dirt around the ball bearing.

Use a bottle brush to get the bottle really clean inside.

Avoiding germs

Don't clean near people's food or dishes. You could clean in the bathroom. Try to disinfect the hamster's things every few weeks with disinfectant used for babies' equipment.

Clean the bathtub or sink when you've finished.

Only use the hamster cleaning equipment for your hamster's things.

Settling back in

When you put your hamster back in its clean cage, it may seem upset. It may rush around with the fresh shavings and bedding in its mouth.

At first, a hamster may refuse to make its bed in a clean cage.

It may rub its scent glands along the side of the cage and wash a lot. Don't worry, it will soon settle down again.

Hamster babies

Hamsters are born in the same way as humans. Their first food is milk, which they drink straight from their mothers.

Syrian hamsters can have twelve or more babies at a time. Dwarfs can have up to eight.

Newborn hamsters

Newborn hamsters have no fur, sight or hearing, but they can smell things. They are about the size of a paperclip.

This is a nest of four-day-old Syrian hamsters.

Growing up

The babies change fast. After two weeks, they have fur, and can see, hear and walk unsteadily. They start feeding on normal hamster food as well as their mother's milk.

The babies start sitting up to clean themselves but often topple over.

Rough and tumble

Baby hamsters tumble around and look as though they are fighting, but they are only playing. They often sleep piled on top of one another, but rarely come to any harm.

Baby hamsters play with their siblings.

Leaving the nest

At three to four weeks old, the babies have to leave their mother. If they stay with her for much longer, she may attack them.

Syrian babies will probably start to fight or mate with one another if they stay together for longer than four weeks.

These Syrians are four weeks old.

They are ready to leave their mother and be adopted as pets.

Full grown

Syrian hamsters are full grown by the time they are three or four months old. Dwarfs are full grown even earlier, at about two months old. From then on, hamsters don't change much in appearance.

This three-month-old Syrian is now grown up.

One parent or two?

Syrian babies are looked after by their mother only. Dwarf hamsters often live in pairs, so both parents may look after the babies.

A dwarf father may carry food to the babies.

Going away

You can leave hamsters on their own for up to two nights, because of the way they store their food. Leave an extra water bottle in the cage if your hamster drinks a lot. Only leave enough fresh food for the first day.

Your hamster will be pleased to have a treat while you are away.

If you are going away for more than two nights, someone will need to come in to feed your hamster. Better still, ask if it can stay at a friend's, or board it at a pet store or vet's.

Going to a friend's

Give instructions to your friend. Write down how much food to give, and which fresh foods. Explain how to clean your hamster's cage out.

Leave your friend everything she will need.

Your friend may want to get your hamster out of its cage. Make sure she knows how to play with it safely, though.

Your hamster mustn't play with another hamster. They may fight or mate. It is best if they can't even smell each other.

Keep two hamsters in separate rooms.

Keeping healthy

Well cared for hamsters don't often become ill. As they get old, they start to slow down and sleep more. If you are ever worried about your hamster, take it to see a vet.

Frozen stiff

If your hamster appears to die in cold weather, it may just be in a very deep sleep. Don't try to wake it quickly. First, move it to a warm place.

Don't squeeze or rub your hamster. Your body heat is enough to warm it.

Then, hold it very gently. The warmth of your body may revive it in an hour or so. Afterwards, make sure it has plenty of extra bedding.

Your hamster will use its extra bedding to burrow into to keep warm.

Upset stomach

If your hamster's droppings are watery, stop giving it fresh food. If it has a bad upset stomach, don't feed it for 24 hours but make sure it drinks plenty of water.

You may need to put the water bottle to your hamster's mouth.

On the move

If your hamster needs to see a vet, you could take it in a small pet carrier like the one in this photograph.

A pair of dwarfs can travel together.

Put some bedding in the carrier.

Index

Cover design by Kate Rimmer
Digital manipulation by Keith Furnival

Photo credits

(t-top, m-middle, b-bottom, l-left, r-right)
All photographs ©Tim Flach and Howard Allman except:
Cover (ml) ©De Meester/ARCO/naturepl.com (br) ©Mark Taylor/naturepl.com;
p4 (m) p20 (bm) ©Arco Images GmbH/Alamy; p11 (tl) ©Jean-Michel Labat/ardea.com

With thanks to Armitage Brothers plc, Rosewood Pet Products Ltd and Rolf C. Hagen
(UK) Ltd for supplying hamster equipment used in photographs.
Thanks also to Jessica Bailey and Nadia Allman.

First published in 2013 by Usborne Publishing Ltd, Usborne House, 83–85 Saffron Hill, London
EC1N 8RT, England. www.usborne.com Copyright © 2013 Usborne Publishing Ltd. The
name Usborne and the devices Ⓤ are Trade Marks of Usborne Publishing Ltd.
All rights reserved. UE. Printed in Dongguan, Guangdong, China.